Illusions Lost

An Elegy in Three Parts

Derryl Hermanutz

Illusions Lost - An Elegy in Three Parts

Copyright 2020 by Derryl Hermanutz

ISBN 9798653443602

Related books by this author:

The Road to Debt Bondage: How Banks Create Unpayable Debt (2018)

How Banks Create Money and Why Governments Should Too (2020)

A Brief History of Financial Plunder (2020)

The paperbacks and ebooks are available at Amazon. A free download of each ebook is available at Smashwords.

Derryl Hermanutz is an independent researcher and writer

Table of Contents

Part 1: A World Without People   4

Part 2: Progress   8

Part 3: Growth   26

Requiem   52

Bibliography   60

Part 1: A World Without People

In 1817 David Ricardo - that great advocate of free trade to exploit the wealth-enhancing benefits of comparative advantage - admitted the Luddites were right. Replacing paid workers with unpaid machines permanently reduces the need for human workers and renders the human population "redundant" to the owners of the machines. {David Ricardo, *Principles of Political Economy and Taxation*, Chapter XXXI On Machinery (1817)}

200 years later we are approaching the logical conclusion of that process. Here's what it looks like.

Machines replace people.

Machines don't "supplement" people.

People are replaced by machines.

The machines now do the things people used to do.

So what are the people going to do, now that they have been replaced by machines?

The people are going to die.

Well, that's the plan, anyway. Or the assumption. Or the hope.

"There are too many people. People are unsustainable. We need less people."

It's a "scientific fact" that a few billion people have to die off or the future will not be sustainable.

The "we" who confidently proclaim these "facts" do not identify as "the people". No, they are the technocrats - the knowing ones; the "smart" ones - who design the machines that replace the people. People are stupid. People are expendable. Technocrats are necessary. And smart.

Technocrats replace unsustainable people with sustainable "smart" machines. The technocrats are not going to die. The technocrats are building the "smart" future. The smart future needs the smart technocrats and doesn't need the stupid people.

What happens to all the unsustainable people whose work has been replaced by machines, but who still need to consume material resources - food, energy, clothes, housing - to survive as living creatures?

They are redundant.

They are unsustainable.

They die off.

Extinction.

An evolutionary extinction event in which homo sapiens - smart humans - are replaced by even smarter machines: mechanico sapiens.

Except this is not Charles Darwin's "accidental" evolution by random mutation and natural selection.

It is Herbert Spencer's Social Darwinism - eugenics; a targeted culling of the herd: deliberate social engineering that willfully sacrifices the people; renders the population redundant, superfluous, expendable.

The machines are not actually "sustainable". Indeed, the machines are the cause of the unsustainability problem.

Human workers are muscle-powered and food-fueled. Food - especially organically grown plant-based food - is a clean green renewable energy source to fuel human workers. Small scale organic farming is knowledge-based and highly productive but labor intensive - economically smart but financially inefficient - so billions of food-fueled humans doing the work of growing food are replaced by millions of giant fossil-fueled machines doing the work of industrial scale corporate agribusiness.

The industrial and agricultural machines are motor-powered and fossil-fueled or electric-fueled. Burning the Earth's limited supply of non-renewable fossil fuels; and digging out the Earth's limited supply of non-renewable natural resources to build the electricity-generating infrastructure and to build all the machines; is polluting the planet and consuming the Earth's non-renewable resources at an unsustainable rate.

Human labor is naturally-fueled, clean, renewable, and sustainable.

Machine labor is artificially-fueled, polluting, non-renewable, and unsustainable.

And the smart machines are not actually "smart".

They are hardware - built in factories; running software programs - written by techies; powered by batteries - made in other factories. When the batteries run down the machines don't die. They are recharged, resurrected from the dead, put back in service doing their gods' work.

The corporations that build and own and employ the machines don't die either. Their human owners and managers come and go, live and die. But the corporations live forever. Except the corporations are not alive. They are legal constructs - a stack of papers in a filing cabinet. The human owners and managers serve the insatiable need of the eternally lifeless legal construct: grow bigger, and profit.

The corporation has a singular mission: maximize profits. Growing bigger maximizes sales revenues. Human workers are a cost. Corporations replace paid workers with unpaid machines to minimize costs and maximize profits. It is the logic of anti-Spock. The needs of the few legal constructs outweigh the needs of the many redundant humans.

The machines (and corporations) are not alive. They are not conscious. They cannot feel, or think, or experience, or know. They do not decide for themselves what they will do - or not do. The machines are neither smart nor stupid. They are manufactured hardware running manufactured software programs. The machines do what they were made to do.

Everything they do is determined by the "smart" technocrats who built and programmed the machines. They wound up their mechanical toy and set it loose. "Look! It's moving by itself! It's alive! It's smart!" The technocrats love their little machines, their progeny, their legacy to the sustainable future.

But technocrats don't love people, because people are unsustainable and redundant. And stupid. Bunch of stupid populists.

The technocrats are the not so smart creator-gods who are building the not actually sustainable future.

The 'smart' machines are their creatures, who will populate the 'smart' future, doing their gods' work.

Non-living, non-feeling, non-thinking creatures.

Dead, soul-less, mindless automatons, mimicking "smart" behavior.

A simulacrum of life and intelligence, acted out by robots running algorithms. Robots that replace intelligent living feeling people.

Technocrats are the gods of the lifeless machines.

Ruling over a world without people.

In their sustainable "smart" future.

Part 2: Progress

200 years ago David Ricardo admitted the Luddites were right: replacing paid workers with unpaid machines permanently reduces the need for human workers and renders the population "redundant" to the owners of machines. Today we are approaching the logical conclusion of that process: a mass die-off of redundant humans; replaced by a world populated with "smart" machines performing their mechanical labors in service to the remnant population of human masters.

Here's the ideological path that delivered us to our oh-so-"smart" present moment in the sun.

Conventional wisdom mocks the Luddites as throwbacks who stand in the way of "progress". Sure, you lost your job working in the buggy whip factory, but now you can go work in Henry Ford's new car factory, for better wages. The economy *always* creates even better jobs, to replace the obsolete jobs that were destroyed by "progress".

One purveyor of the conventional wisdom - Joseph Schumpeter - even invented a name for this ideological certainty: creative destruction. You destroy the old and crappy jobs, to make way for all the new and better jobs. Everybody wins! It's a "fact".

The Luddites were wrong about machinery, says the conventional wisdom. The Luddites were better off, after their manual labor jobs were replaced by machines. They got even better jobs.

No, we didn't get even better jobs, or any other jobs, reply the Luddites. But the conventional wisdom can't hear the Luddites because they are saying something that the conventional wisdom knows is "impossible". Everybody gets better jobs. It's a "fact". Luddites are stupid populists who don't understand "smart" economic theory.

Ricardo recognized that mechanization always creates *less* new jobs than it destroys old jobs, and constantly eliminates the need for human workers, and "deteriorates the condition of the laborer"...which the Luddites *knew* was the case, because their condition was indeed deteriorating.

The Luddites were not proposing a theory. They were objecting to their real life loss of livelihood and intensifying material immiseration, which is the "question" that economists were theorizing about. The economists were not observing Luddites. The economists were looking at their theories about the effects of mechanization on the working class masses.

The dominant theory was that everybody's material condition is improved by the financial "efficiencies" of mechanization. Human workers are a cost, so by supplementing or replacing paid workers with unpaid machines, the capitalists who own the productive businesses can produce the same or greater outputs at a lower cost price per unit.

Workers will be able to buy more stuff with their earned incomes, because producers' cost price is reduced; and competition among producers ensures they pass on their cost savings by selling their stuff to consumers at lower prices. More financially efficient production, that produces stuff at lower cost with less paid human workers, enables everybody to enjoy buying lots of cheap stuff. It's a fact!

But workers whose jobs were *replaced* by machines - not "supplemented" by machines - are earning no spendable incomes at all. "Everyday low prices" are moot, to people who have no money to pay any prices. In a market economy where stuff is produced for sale and everything is bought-sold for money, if you have no income and no money, you can't buy any stuff. Like food. So you die.

Ricardo had previously believed in the conventional wisdom, so he "saw" - in his mind - that it was logically impossible for workers' lives to be immiserated when their jobs were replaced by machines. If it's logically impossible then it can't be real, no matter how much real-life evidence the Luddites present to empirically demonstrate that it is indeed real.

People who believe in theories see what they believe, and can't see things that are "impossible". The Luddites were just imagining their immiseration. Slackers and whiners. No basis in "sound" economic theory and logic.

Then Ricardo figured out how it could be logically possible that even as the net income (capitalists' profits) of a nation increased, the gross income (capitalists' profits + workers' wages; wages are capitalists' costs) could decrease.

Capitalists own the machines, pay workers' wages as their costs, and sell the outputs to earn their sales revenues. Sales revenues minus costs = profits. GDP is total sales revenues: total stuff produced and bought-sold. Total sales revenue is a nation's gross income: workers' wages + owners' profits. Owners' profits is net income.

By replacing paid workers with unpaid machines, the capitalists could sell the same or more units of stuff, with a lower cost price per unit, and a lower sale price per unit. Total sales revenues (GDP: units of stuff sold times price per unit) can decrease, but if capitalists' costs (workers' wages) have decreased by even more; then capitalists actually earn more profits (their own incomes) even as national GDP declines.

After Ricardo saw how it was logically possible for capitalist-owned machines to create structural unemployment and damage the interests of the now permanently unemployed and impoverished workers, Ricardo could "see" that it was actually happening.

So what happens to the Luddites - the unemployed workers whose paid jobs were replaced by unpaid machines in order to maximize capitalists' profits? They are no longer being paid incomes for working, so they no longer have money to buy their daily necessities of life.

Ricardo was clear, "I am convinced that the substitution of machinery for human labor is very often injurious to the interest of the class of laborers."

But, like his fellow classical economists, Ricardo's only advice to the working class was to stop breeding because you are producing an excessive oversupply of redundant workers.

Too many people; not enough jobs.

The purpose of life is to work, not to live.

The purpose of the productive economy is to generate money profits for owners, not to produce material necessities for consumers.

A business invests money as its costs and earns money as its sales revenues. Sales revenues minus costs = profits. Business owners ("capitalists") invest their own money as their costs, earn the sales revenues as their business income, and earn the profits as their personal income; or owners pay the business losses out of their own pockets.

If a business fails to earn profits, and loses its owner's money, the business dies. The owner voluntarily euthanizes the money-losing business; shuts it down to stop the bleeding, to stop losing even more of the owner's money.

Businesses are productive entities. People are productive entities. If an entity loses money it must be euthanized to stop the losses. Money losing entities have to die.

If you are a money losing entity - if you don't work and earn money, but you still spend money buying food - you shouldn't live either. You should die.

Old school morality. Puritan. Biblical, even, depending on which parts of the Bible you choose to quote. It's a big book. It says lots of sh*t. Some sayings contradict other sayings. What are the faithful to believe, who read the book, and are given conflicting advice? They believe what they choose to believe, and don't believe the rest.

Puritans chose old school Leviticus morality: a pound of flesh no more no less; an eye for an eye and a tooth for a tooth; and rejected Jesus' advice to turn the other cheek, and give what you can to those who need it more than you do. Old school Hebrew prophets like Isaiah (around 600 BC) said the same things Jesus said, centuries before Jesus said it.

Leviticus Chapter 25 describes the Jubilee Year in which debts are forgiven, land is returned to its former owners, and slaves are freed from debt bondage. Maybe Puritans only read the first 24 chapters of Leviticus - the "good" parts; and refused to read the "bad" parts that say forgive us our debts, as we forgive our debtors. Which Jesus said, too, centuries later. No point reading that socialist crap! God helps him who helps himself, and devil take the hindmost. That's what the Good Book says, yessiree. It's a fact!

In his 1992 Earth Charter, Maurice Strong wanted to "change the hearts and minds of humanity" to end greedy self-serving old school morality and usher in planet-preserving and humanity-serving new school morality. Isaiah said the same words, 2600 years before Maurice Strong wrote them, and the same words were repeated by John (John 12:39-40) 700 years after Isaiah.

Here's what Isaiah said,

"Go and tell this people:
Be ever hearing but never understanding;
be ever seeing but never perceiving.
Make the heart of this people calloused;
make their ears dull
and close their eyes.
Otherwise they might see with their eyes,
hear with their ears,
understand with their hearts,
and turn, and be healed."
Isaiah 6:9-10

Still, the hearts and minds of humanity's rulers have not changed - they have not "turned, and been healed" - and the ruled masses of humans still suffer the same predations: poverty, asset seizure, debt bondage.

"The Lord enters into judgment against the elders and leaders of his people: It is you who have ruined my vineyard; the plunder from the poor is in your houses. What do you mean by crushing my people, and grinding the faces of the poor?" (Isaiah 3:14-15)

That was 2600 years ago. The more things change...

God helps him who helps himself, chant the Puritans. Being rich is a sign of election, God's assurance to his Chosen that you are one of the "elect" who will be redeemed at the Judgment, rather than condemned to hellfire and damnation. On your deathbed all you have to do is say the magic word Jesus! and you are saved! no matter how much of a greedy self-serving hypocritical b*stard you were all your life.

It's not written anywhere in the Bible, that God favors rich people and being rich assures you of eternal life. That idea is a tenet of the Puritan faith in market economy and market morality.

Jesus - whose sayings *are* written in the Bible - said being rich is more likely evidence that you serve the "other" god - the money-loving god Mammon. Jesus said you cannot serve both God and Mammon. {Matthew 6:24; Luke 16:13} God is Spirit. Service to God means living by spiritual values: loving, true understanding, giving what you can to those who need it. You can't get rich, if you give your money and stuff to people who need it more than you do. Giving, and accumulating, are mutually exclusive.

600 years before Jesus, Isaiah said the same thing about greedy accumulation that deprives everybody else of the property that they need to live, "Woe to you who add house to house and join field to field till no space is left and you live alone in the land." (Isaiah 5:8)

In the 1930s Upton Sinclair observed, "It is difficult to get a man to understand something, when his salary depends upon his not understanding it." Willful self-delusion - the rejection of clear seeing and true understanding - to avoid seeing the life-destroying planet-destroying things you have to do in order to get paid money; and a hardened heart to avoid being moved by compassionate generosity to spend your wealth to ameliorate the need and suffering of other living, feeling creatures - or at least let them keep the property they need in order to earn their own living.

Mammon is service to money, and all the things money can buy. Service to Mammon means living by material values: taking; getting richer; take what you can get, and devil take the hindmost.

Whose values are served by market morality? God's? or Mammon's?

In his 1944 book, *The Great Transformation: The Political and Economic Origins of Our Time*, Karl Polanyi described the 19th century processes by which citizens of Christian nations under God and King were transformed into producers and consumers within market economy under the invisible hand of the marketplace. {Polanyi observed that the invisible hand is connected to the more visible arms and bodies of international bankers who control nations' access to money by owning the bond market. But we'll leave that matter alone for now.}

The dominant worldview of Western society was successfully transformed. The perceptions, values and beliefs of the people and rulers of the nations changed with it.

"Society" transformed into "economy".

People with "souls", hungry for salvation, became people with "bodies", hungry for stuff.

People became consumers, lovers and buyers of stuff.

Spiritual values are imaginary.

I want money, that's what I want.

Money buys stuff. Stuff is "real", physical. I can buy it and own it and haul it home and store it in my garage. I can go look at it, to confirm it's real, and still there, not robbed by some crook!

Having stuff is good.

Not having stuff is bad.

There must be something wrong with you, if you don't have stuff.

Sinner.

Poor person.

Slave to your immoral vices.

Your vices made you poor, you sinner, violator of the moral order.

Virtue makes you rich. Rich people are virtuous. Poor people are vicious.

Jesus said the opposite, but Jesus was replaced by market economy. Souls are imaginary. Bodies are real. Jesus is imaginary. Market economy is real. So Jesus doesn't count.

Market values replaced Christian values.

Christian nations became market economies.

The religious priesthood was replaced by a secular priesthood. Economists are now the High Priests who tell us the gods' truths about who and what we are and how the world works; and tell us what is true and good and right, and what is not.

Classical economists told the redundant working class masses that the gods of this world had no need for the likes of them, and that is why they were destitute and suffering. So die. And stop breeding more suffering laborers whom the gods of this world have no use for.

Except the economists weren't actually speaking to the redundant masses.

The laboring masses were largely illiterate, or only read snippets of the Bible, and didn't know what the classical economists were writing and saying to each other, and saying to the owners and rulers of the nations. The masses didn't know they were redundant. Nobody told them. So how could they do the right thing and die off? They didn't know they were "supposed to", according to the certainly true axioms and valid internal logic of market morality.

In his 1848 book, *Principles of Political Economy,* John Stuart Mill also recognized that mechanized production produces plenty of stuff, but the earned income system of distributing purchasing power fails at adequately distributing the stuff to the people who need and want it. Mill advocated a more political, less market distribution of the fruits of industrial production, to provide a subsistence to people who didn't "earn it" by working. Mill also recommended less breeding of more redundant workers; and advocated pursuing a steady state economy rather than an endless growth economy.

Karl Marx and Friedrich Engels had a different solution: eliminate capitalists; which they proposed in *The Communist Manifesto*, published the same year (1848) as Mill's book.

In the 1920s and 30s CH Douglas proposed yet another solution to the same economic distribution problem, with his social credit money and price system that featured government-issued money to fund a National Dividend paid to every citizen as their "cultural inheritance"; and to fund a subsidy paid to the owners of productive businesses so they could still have spendable personal incomes while selling their goods to consumers at money-losing below-cost prices.

But none of these reform proposals managed to unseat market economy's moral imperative that all spendable income must be earned, all production must be money-profitable; and those who spend more than they earn must surely die.

Nevertheless, Mill, a child of Enlightenment faith in material and spiritual progress that leads to the "perfection" of human nature, foresaw a future in which mechanization of work would free much of humanity from the curse of Adam - "By the sweat of thy brow you will eat your food until you return to the ground." (Genesis 3:19) - which would provide people with free time to develop their "higher" intellectual, moral and spiritual natures.

Indeed, the internet today makes the accumulated knowledge of humanity instantly available to anybody, anywhere, via the hand-held supercomputers we call "smartphones". But just because this vast wealth of knowledge is "available", does not mean everybody or anybody actually "avails" themselves of it.

We see today what the masses of people actually do when they do not have to spend their days toiling at physical labors. They learn how to use "smart" phones so they can text OMG! to each other, and take selfies of their *ss to post on social media. Einstein observed that as technology gets smarter, people get stupider. Smart phones and *ss selfies are not what the Enlightenment foresaw as humanity's material and spiritual "progress".

Today's secular priesthood is less forthright than its classical forebears.

Economists today assure laid off workers that they will get "even better jobs" in the new clean green economy. But those human workers are redundant to the productive economy, which is populated by machines. In factories, human welders are replaced by robotic welders. In infrastructure, one large backhoe permanently replaces 500 human ditch diggers.

Economists assure the laid off ditch diggers that they will become robotics engineers and app developers in the new "knowledge" economy. Some people even believe that fairy tale.

Back here in the real world, algorithms are replacing knowledge workers a lot faster than industrial machines ever replaced trades and crafts workers. By the time the ditch diggers have finished their schooling to become robotics engineers, those jobs will no longer exist. "Smart" robots will be doing those jobs. All that's left for humans is the student debt, and the redundant workers, with no jobs, and no incomes to pay their debts.

Machines replace - permanently eliminate the need for - human workers. Ricardo knew that. Mill hoped it would happen.

In any event, it happened. And permanent structural unemployment ensued.

During the 19th and early 20th centuries, industrializing Europe shipped off millions of its redundant population to colonize the New World. In the 20th century, 10s of millions of working age men and women were killed in World Wars. The Spanish flu (1918-1920) killed 10s of millions more.

None of those millions of off-shored and dead workers ever got "even better jobs" in Europe's industrial economy. They were redundant. So they were shipped off to conquer and colonize new lands; lands that had not yet been converted into "property"; undeveloped lands that capitalists did not yet own, but would soon enough own, after the millions of off-shored workers had done the work of "developing" the lands.

Or the redundant populations were given guns and shipped off to kill each other in Wars, by the millions. Industrial scale carnage. But lots of work rebuilding the blown up nations. Work is virtuous. Sloth is sinful. Hurray! for Wars that create work for millions!

There are no more 'empty' continents to off-shore redundant workers. Space technology has not yet scaled up to off-planet today's billions of redundant workers to colonize Mars and the habitable planets of the Milky Way galaxy, populating brave new worlds with the future's supply of surplus humans. World War 3 is still an option to kill off 100s of millions...or billions, if the war goes nuclear.

Viral pandemics like the Spanish flu can kill off a significant percentage of the human population in a year or two. But viruses also kill the "smart" and "necessary" and "rich" people, not just the redundant slackers. ...until "smart" viruses are built and unleashed, to kill only stupid poor people and leave the smart rich ones alive to inhabit the New World Order.

Off-shoring, and killing off, have historically been the policies of choice to deal with redundant populations of surplus laborers who fail to cease breeding more surplus laborers.

Classical economists like Ricardo were at least honest enough to admit that industrial capitalism does not need all those humans as workers.

Productive businesses - especially large corporations - continue to invest in machines to replace human workers. You buy the machine once, and you never have to pay it again. People have to be continuously paid for the work they do. It is financially inefficient -

unprofitable - to continue paying human workers who could be replaced by unpaid machines.

As financial enterprises, businesses are in business to maximize sales revenues and minimize costs in order to maximize business owners' profits. People - human workers - are a cost. So wherever possible, paid workers are replaced with unpaid machines.

In the sphere of economic production, the businesses who own the machines and produce the stuff are in the business of rendering human workers redundant.

Which they continue doing today, as they have been doing for the past 2 1/2 centuries.

While the economic priesthood continues to preach the gospel of "even better jobs" that never materialize for the redundant masses.

Permanently unemployed people have no incomes to spend buying all the stuff the businesses so efficiently produce with their unpaid machines.

Unpaid machines don't buy stuff.

So how can the businesses sell all the stuff they produce, and earn profits, if a large portion of the consumer population earns no incomes from working?

The short answer is - debt.

Ever-increasing totals of household and government debt.

The debts are permanently unpayable.

Commercial banks create new money - spendable deposit account balances; to purchase new interest-bearing debts - debtor's new loan account debt balances and bond debts. Debtors' interest-bearing debts are banks' interest-earning assets. Debtors spend the new deposit account balances, which debtors owe back to the banks as payment of their new loan account and bond debt balances. Meanwhile, as long as the debts remain unpaid, debtors pay interest on their unpaid debt balances, and banks earn the interest payments as their business income from their money creation and lending business.

People can spend more money than they earn; and governments can spend more money than they tax; and businesses can earn more money in sales revenues than the spendable and taxable earned incomes they paid out as their costs; because of the miracle of commercial bank money creation and lending.

Well, the word "miracle" may be too strong, or optimistic.

Bamboozlement? Accounting chicanery? Ponzi arithmetic? The magical art of putting a $ sign in front of a number to create money out of nothing and lend it to debtors at interest? The black art of creating equal negative $numbers that condemn their possessors to debtors' purgatory, or hell? Sinners. Debtors. Damn them all to hell. They should have got even better jobs!

A variety of slipshod makeshift 'solutions' - to the insufficient spendable earned incomes and unpayable debts problems - have been implemented, against powerful opposition from market moralists who insist all spendable money must be earned and if you don't work you don't eat. You die off. You were supposed to get an even better job, you slacker. Charles Darwin (I mean Herbert Spencer) has ways of ensuring the likes of you don't survive to pollute the gene pool with more slackers. Dog kills dog. Survival of the vicious.

But people dying off from destitution in "developed" countries makes life uncomfortable for politicians who are titularly responsible for the public welfare.

The economic priesthood had assured the population that everybody benefits from the efficiencies of privately owned market economy that generates "progress" driven by the profit motive. Dying of poverty is not a "benefit". Even stupid populists know that much.

And there are millions of them, stupid populists, with no jobs and no incomes, destitute. Sinners. If they have nothing left to lose - if they lose faith in market economy, and stop believing in the comforting assurances of the economic priesthood - who knows what kinds of mischief they might get up to in their death throes.

So governments implement tax-and-redistribute welfare programs that take money from people and businesses who earned it by working, and give the money to people who don't work...because there is no work for them, because they live in market economy where workers are systematically replaced by machines to maximize owners' profits.

Taxpayers oppose paying taxes, and avoid and evade paying taxes, and resent the recipients of tax-funded welfare programs - the poor people; the morally defective; the unemployed slackers; the redundant masses who refuse to get even better jobs and who are given taxpayers' money so they can continue to buy food and eat and enjoy their work-free lives of splendid leisure in the everyday low price slums of the Earth.

A large portion of the tax money is spent paying the political and welfare bureaucracy, people who are themselves being paid for doing make-work jobs that do not produce any economic value that can be sold in the marketplace.

In market economy, all values are money values. If you can't put a money price on it and sell it to a willing buyer in the marketplace, then it is worthless. How much will you pay me for my human values? my spiritual values? my social or environmental values? You won't pay me any money for my values? Then all those values are worthless, and don't "count" in market economy.

If you can't sell it to a willing buyer who spends his/her own money in the marketplace, it has "no value", and you can't "earn" any money by doing that kind of make-work.

That's what market moralists say. Many of them believe it's "true"...even though it's a value judgment that cannot be objectively true or false, because it depends on what you subjectively "value", and what you don't value.

If you believe the purpose of life is to work, not to live, and you value work over life, then you have built the proper moral foundation for market morality. If you don't work, then you "should" die, according to the logic of market morality. It's a morally constructed "should" that some people believe in. It is not an objective "fact" of reality that everybody can see by looking at it.

If you believe we make our own purposes; or if you believe the purpose of life is to live and develop our physical, mental and moral/spiritual nature - and work is only contingently necessary to support life; then we will fundamentally disagree about what is morally right and wrong, and about how "society" - the human social and economic world - "should" be organized.

Market morality - which is the morality of today's dominant Western worldview - insists that everybody must contribute to economic production because the world suffers "scarcity", so if some people don't work, there will not be enough production to satisfy everybody's needs.

Even though the world's container ship fleets and warehouses and retail stores, and our houses and garages and storage units and garbage dumps, are filled to bursting and overflowing with stuff that has already been produced and continues to be mass produced; market moralists - and the economic priesthood - assure us we are living in economic "scarcity" where there is not enough stuff being produced.

Market moralists see what they believe - scarcity! and cannot see what they don't believe - material abundance.

Market moralists rule, because they won the ideological battle to construct the worldview and the conventional wisdom that the rulers live by. Market moralists - the economic priesthood - are the "experts". The authorities. Are *you* the authorities? Then shut up and believe in what the authorities preach. Scarcity!!!

So everybody has to work at producing more stuff, to justify getting paid money for contributing to production, in order to earn money to spend buying their share of the oh-so-scarce stuff.

Nevertheless, contrary to the dictates of market morality, governments do tax-and-redistribute welfare programs to keep the unemployed masses alive by giving them taxpayers' money to spend paying their costs of living.

And governments, corporations - and quasi-government/quasi corporate institutions (like NGOs and mercenary armies) - create millions of make-work jobs, many of which are outright "bullshit jobs" (David Graeber's term) that do not even appear to be useful or productive; but which nevertheless pay spendable 'earned' incomes to the millions of bullshit workers.

In Graeber's survey, 70% of bullshit workers agreed the world would be a better place if their bullshit jobs did not exist. The victims of mercenary armies would probably agree the world would be a better place if mercenaries' jobs did not exist. The victims of NGO regime change propaganda and civil strife would probably agree the world would be a better place if capitalist-funded NGOs did not exist.

Many people believe humans need to work, not just to get paid money, but to develop our human abilities. Apparently, most of the bullshit workers believe this too, because they are living it, and they know *their* world would be a better place if they weren't.

People stagnate in make-work and bullshit jobs, where all the managers learn is how to pretend they are not flushing money into bottomless pits and not begging for more money to "fund" the pits; and all the workers learn is how to appease their managers' egos and pretend to be doing something constructive. {Meanwhile, all the bullshit managers and workers line up at the bottom of the pit on payday to collect the money that is being dumped into the hole. Money is paid to people, not paid to holes in the ground.}

Spending your days like that is a complete waste of time and life. Soul destroying. Depressing. Futile. But the bullshit workers don't quit their soul-destroying bullshit jobs, because the jobs pay incomes, which the people need in order to pay their monthly cost of living spending.

Within market economy, people sell their souls to get money. They have to. They need the money. Or else they die.

Money - which buys everything you need and want - is the most basic necessity of life, within buy-sell for money market economy.

If you have no money you can't buy food, or pay your rent and utilities, or your mortgage and car loan, or your property taxes, or your student loan and credit card payment.

So your electricity and water and phone and cable and internet get shut off. You get evicted from your house for non-payment of your rent or mortgage or property taxes. You can't buy food. You will be hounded and hunted by collection agencies to squeeze the last drop of money out of your flat broke *ss. We cannot live without money to pay for our daily necessities of life - our cost of living spending.

The cost of living money is paid to the landlords and service providers and merchants who rent housing and sell utility services and food and other necessities (and small luxuries like booze and dope) to the consumers. And the money is paid to the banks as interest on the bank loans and credit card debts that enable consumers to spend more money than they earn, which enables businesses and landlords to earn the additional money as higher rents and additional sales revenues.

And the money is spent paying interest to banks on mortgage loans - newly created deposit account balances - that enables the construction and real estate industry to earn sales revenues by selling houses to debt-financed buyers who cannot afford to buy $300,000 houses with their savings. Because most people have no savings, or have a pittance of savings - maybe enough to pay their costs of living until the end of the week, or the end of the month, or the next 3-4 months. Then they have no money.

People depend on "having incomes"; not on "having money". Most people - the god-forsaken morally defective sinners condemned to suffer in this life and hellfire and damnation in the next for failing to be rich Chosen Ones - have a scarcity of spendable incomes; and a worse scarcity of spendable savings.

There is no scarcity of houses to buy or rent; and stores full of stuff to buy. There is no scarcity of productive businesses, and workers and suppliers, who are ready to go to work producing a lot more new houses and every other kind of stuff, if somebody will pay them to do it.

There is a scarcity of spendable incomes to pay for the stuff. So banks create and lend new money to debtors, who spend the new money buying all the houses and cars and college educations and "smart" phones and other stuff, which enables producers of all that stuff to sell it, and get paid the new money.

But debt has to be repaid out of future earned incomes.

Which brings us to Part 3 of this elegy, the need for constant, exponentially increasing debt-financed economic growth to prevent mass debtor defaults, banking system failure, Collapse of the banks' debt-based money system, and Collapse of the capitalists' buy-sell for money market economy.

But it's going to Collapse anyway, because the planet cannot support unlimited growth of production and consumption of the Earth's abundant - but limited - supply of natural resources to convert into stuff for sale.

When the global industrial economy runs out of economically accessible fossil fuels to burn, fossil-fueled industrial civilization is finished.

And so are we, whose lives as consumers depend on the fossil-fueled industrial production and transportation system continuing to deliver everything we need and want from far-flung producers "to a retailer near you".

Part 3: Growth

Planet of the Humans - the new docu-movie by Michael Moore and Jeff Gibbs - graphically highlights the realities of the limits to growth and the delusion of green growth and green energy.

The Empire of Illusion has launched a desperate counterattack, all guns blazing to shoot ideological bullets at the visible truth to preserve billionaires' expectation of earning trillions of corporate sales revenues and profits by consuming what's left of the Earth's resources to build and install, and own and operate, the physical infrastructure of the Fourth Industrial Revolution: "the 5G internet of things" - while maintaining the mass delusion that *this* Industrial Revolution is "virtual", not "physical".

There is no such thing as "clean" growth or clean energy. Economic activity is "physical". Growth requires consuming evermore physically-generated energy to intensify our industrial exploitation of this planet's physical resources, and intensify polluting it with our physical waste.

To build the new green clean energy "smart" cities of the future will require vast amounts of energy to produce billions of tons of concrete and steel and glass and copper and aluminum and plastics and other materials. Where are those billions of tons of physical materials going to come from, and how will they be transported from the remote mines that produce them to the "smart" cities that use them?

Green utopians are confident that technological innovation will enable ongoing economic growth and material wealth accumulation, while reducing or eliminating our need to ravage the planet's material resources and pollute it with our physical wastes. Technological innovation is a fact!

In the utopian future, smart 3D printers will build the green energy infrastructure and smart cities "out of nothing", using zero natural resources and zero dirty energy. The smart printers will not work by technologies based on advanced "something out of nothing" physics (that doesn't exist) but by magic (that doesn't exist either).

The clean green "smart" future exists as a faith-based fantasy in the minds of green utopians. Economic activity in the real industrial world is physical, energy and resource consuming, and polluting. Green utopians believe what they imagine and deny the realities of physical reality.

Delusion runs deep, when there is no realistic hope of sustaining "growth" - or even of maintaining our present level of economic consumption and waste - without destroying what's left of the planet.

Market economy itself creates the need for never-ending growth to provide never-ending profits to the never-dying corporations that own the productive economy. To end the need for environmentally unsustainable economic growth requires ending our slavish servitude to the delusory worldview of market economy. It probably requires ending the corporate ownership and private economic government system. And it requires changing the way money is created and allocated.

As long as money - $numbers that are created out of nothing in unlimited amounts - is treated as a "scarce commodity" that must be "earned"; while the planet is treated as a "free" supply of unlimited resources and an unlimited capacity garbage dump: there will be no end to the intensifying destruction of the natural world in order to produce and sell evermore stuff to "earn" evermore of the created-out-of-nothing money.

As long as money is issued as a private monopoly by commercial banks to serve the banks' profit needs; rather than issued by governments as a public utility to serve the economy's money needs: no beneficial solutions to all of the other problems will be financially "affordable" - for lack of enough numbers with a $ sign in front of them to pay the people and businesses who design and implement the solutions.

Paying people and businesses to clean up the oceans is money-losing, not money-profitable, because nobody "owns" the oceans so nobody will pay you for doing the job of cleaning them up. You spend money paying the people who do the work; but you don't earn any money by getting the job done; so you lose money. The production of public goods - like public infrastructure, social welfare, and a clean environment - is money losing; not money profitable.

If you - the government - can't issue your own money to pay the people to do the job of producing money losing public goods; and if banks won't create and lend you the money because it is a money-losing venture and you will earn no sales revenues and no profits to pay the loan interest and repay the loan principal; and if capital markets investors won't lend you the money for the same reasons banks won't; and if taxpayers cannot afford to pay for the job because they already earn too little spendable incomes and owe too many payable debts; and if rich people won't pay for the job because they want to keep their money and stay rich, not spend their money and get poor: then there will be "no money" to pay for the environmentally beneficial but money-losing enterprise of cleaning up the oceans.

[...unless the oceans are "privatized" - in which case "philanthrocapitalists" will offer to pay for cleaning up the oceans, in exchange for being granted ownership and control of the oceans, so they can then charge tolls to everybody who uses the oceans, so the owners can then earn profits by owning the oceans.

That is: philanthrocapitalists will offer to *invest* their money *buying the oceans* to own as their private profit-generating assets; while pretending to be performing a "public service" by *spending* their money to do the job at their own expense.

Investing your money to buy ownership and control of assets is called "capitalism". Spending or giving away your money for the benefit of others is called "philanthropy". Philanthro-capitalism is a contradiction in terms.]

There are lots of smart engineers who have figured out various ways of doing the job of cleaning up the oceans. It's a huge job. It will cost billions. There are plenty of unemployed and under-employed people and businesses ready, willing and able to do the work. They all need money to pay their cost of living spending, and to pay their debts. They are anxious to be hired to do the job. But if there is no money to pay them, nobody gets hired, and the job does not get done.

In buy-sell for money market economy that uses bank-issued repayable money - and uses investors' invested money - all large scale economic endeavors must be money-profitable, or they don't happen, because the people and businesses who do the work cannot afford to do the job "for free", and banks and investors need and want to earn their invested money back, with interest.

If governments issued the money to pay for the job, the workers would be hired and paid, and the job would get done, and the workers and businesses would have money to pay their own expenses and paydown their debts, and the government would lose money, but so what?

Money is numbers that are created out of nothing - either by banks, or by governments. Bank-issued money is "debt-based", which means it has to be paid back to the banks. Government-issued money can be "debt-free", which means it doesn't have to be paid back to the government; and the government doesn't have to collect future taxes to get money to pay the money back "to itself".

Government spending of its own debt-free money can pay for the production of money losing public goods, which simultaneously provides the private sector economy with a supply of money to use to pay its own spending, and to paydown its debts owed to banks.

The world doesn't need evermore stuff. More effective *use* of stuff - distributed to people who need it, not to people who simply pile it up until they run out of storage space then throw the stuff away - eliminates the need for "more stuff".

More effective use of stuff requires more effective distribution of the spendable money that buys the stuff. Which means governments creating debt-free money and giving a minimum monthly amount of un-earned income to everybody so they can pay for a minimal cost of living spending; and ending banks' power to create debt-based money out of nothing and lend it to debt-finance consumer spending.

The result would be less production of needless stuff sold to debt-financed but materially extravagant and wasteful consumers, and better distribution of necessary stuff sold to people who spend their minimum monthly incomes buying the necessities.

"Savers" don't waste their money buying needless stuff. Savers spend some of their income buying what they need, and save the rest. Savers 'buy' their own financial security by saving their money.

But people who already spent all of their earned incomes buying the stuff they need, are happy to buy more stuff they don't need, if somebody will lend them the money to pay for it. And they will keep buying more stuff they don't need until their credit gets cut off. Then they will default on paying their debts, because they only earn enough money to pay for what they need, and don't earn extra money to pay back their debts.

Household debt is at historic highs. The debt-financed consumers may be making their interest payments, but they are never going to be able to repay the loan principal money and will end up defaulting; so the banks are effectively giving them "free money" to waste buying needless stuff.

Taxpayers are going to end up bailing out the money-losing (bankrupt) banks who can't collect the money they are owed by debtors who can't pay their debts. Or savers' deposit account balances are going to be bailed in and written off, to restore solvency to the insolvent banks. Or savers' money will be written off by bankruptcy Trustees, if the banks are allowed to fail.

So ultimately, taxpayers and savers will pay for consumers' debt-financed buying of needless junk that wastes the planet's resources while enriching the profit-earning producers who sell the junk to the debt-financed buyers; and enriching the interest-earning creditor-banks by bailing them out after the debtors default on repaying the loan principal.

That's not how the conventional wisdom says it works. But that's what has historically happened in the real world. And it's what's happening again, right now.

Economic growth is not *physically* necessary.

But within buy-sell for money market economy in which stuff is produced for sale to earn money profits, and the money is issued by for-profit commercial banks as repayable loans at interest, growth is *financially* necessary to prevent systemic debtor default, banking system failure, Debt Deflation Depression, and monetary-cum-economic Collapse.

A capitalist market economy - where all the stuff is produced, and all the money is created, by private for-profit industrial and banking corporations - has to grow or it will Collapse; stop working; shut down and do nothing.

Money is not issued as a public utility to serve the economy's money needs. Money is issued as the banks' private monopoly, to serve the banks' profit needs.

Monetary system reformers over the past century have clearly and repeatedly shown why the banks' debt-based money system can't work; and why government issuance of debt-free money is the solution. "Free" money!? What kind of communist crap is that!!! All money must be earned! The road to hellfire and damnation is paved with free money!

Hyperinflation!!! Weimar!!! Zimbabwe!!! shriek the market moralists - who believe in the delusion that money is produced by the economy, and don't know money is created by banks. The shrieking drowns out any possibility of rational discussion of the debt-free money solution to the failings of debt-based money. The solution is simple and obvious, once you stop shrieking mindlessly, and actually look at it.

Banks create the money and lend it to debtors who spend the money into circulation by paying the new money to a "payee" - somebody who sold something (goods; services - including employees' work of all kinds; assets) to the debtor. The payee was paid and now owns the new bank loan money. Payees re-spend and re-invest some of the money - pay it to the next payees - and payees hold some of the money out of circulation as their savings. Most of the new money is almost immediately earned by a payee - a person or a corporation - who saves the money rather than re-spending or re-investing it.

The total money supply is increasing, because banks are creating new money and debtors are spending it into circulation. But the circulating money supply is decreasing, because payees are continuously earning money out of the spend-earn stream and holding the money out of circulation as their accumulations of financial wealth and security: their money savings.

There is nothing wrong with saving the money you earn.

But the bank loan money supply creation system cannot accommodate saving.

The banks' debt-based money supply creation monopoly sets up a classic fallacy of composition - a "paradox of thrift" - in which behavior that is beneficial for individuals (saving some of the money you earn rather than re-spending it all) is catastrophic for the system as a whole.

Debtors owe all the money back to the banks as payment of their loan account and bond debts. But if payees are saving most of the money - not spending or investing the money into the producer-consumer economy where debtors could earn it back by getting paid for working or by selling the stuff they produce; and where governments can get money by taxing people's and businesses' earned incomes - debtors can't earn (or tax) back the money, so debtors can't pay their loan account and bond debts.

All of the bank loan money still exists. But debtors don't have the money. Debtors spent the money. Payees have all the money. And payees are saving most of it, not spending it, so debtors can't earn it back. So debtors can't pay it back to their creditor banks.

To prevent mass debtor defaults that bankrupts the creditor banks, evermore new debtors have to borrow and spend evermore new bank loan money into circulation, so old debtors can earn enough of the new money to make (most of) their bank loan and bond debt payments. When credit-debt growth slows or stalls, not enough new money is being spent into circulation, debtors default en masse, and there is a "financial crisis" of creditors' uncollectable money that is owed as debtors' unpayable debts.

Most savings are held as deposit balances in bank savings accounts, not cash in safes. Banks don't lend out savers' deposit account balances. Every bank loan and bond purchase is funded by the bank's creation of a brand new bank deposit - a number typed into the Credits column of the debtors' bank deposit accounts. The Credit adds to the debtor's spendable bank deposit account "balance".

Debtors spend their new bank loans and bond sale proceeds.

Debtors pay the new balances to payees - by check, direct deposit, online banking, debit card, etc - within the bank-operated payments system of debiting payer account balances and crediting payee account balances.

The new balances are debited (subtracted) out of the debtors' bank deposit accounts and credited (added) into the first payees' bank deposit accounts.

That's where the deposit account money supply - the spendable, investible, savable (and cashable) "balances" in our bank deposit accounts - comes from, in the first place.

Then payees create the spendable cash money supply when we make cash withdrawals and pay with debits to our deposit account balances.

[The government or central bank doesn't print cash money and spend it into circulation. Currency is sold into the economy via the central and commercial banks.

Commercial banks buy currency (banknotes) from the central bank and pay with debits to their central bank reserve account balances. The central bank "issues" - creates out of nothing - the base money supply: commercial banks' reserve account balances and vault cash.

{"Reserve" accounts are just banks' bank accounts at the central bank; in the same way our "deposit" accounts are our bank accounts in commercial banks; in the same way our "cash" accounts are our bank accounts in shadow banks (e.g. brokerages). The bank account "balances" are numbers in bank accounts, nothing more.}

33

Commercial banks issue the spendable money supply - deposit account balances and cash withdrawals - to the money using economy: people, businesses, governments. Commercial banks issue - create out of nothing - the deposit account balances. Commercial banks buy the banknotes from the central bank, then sell the cash money to their deposit account customers, who pay for our currency purchases with debits to our deposit account balances.]

The spendable money supply begins its existence as the deposit account money supply in debtors' bank deposit accounts. Debtors pay the new balances to payees. Then payees create the spendable cash money supply when we make cash withdrawals and hold our money outside the banking system in the form of banknotes in our pockets.

But most bank deposits are never cashed out. Only 2-5% of the total money supply is the cash money supply in our pockets and cash registers and safes.

Most of the spendable, investible, savable money supply (about 95-98%) never exists in any other form than balances in payees' bank deposit accounts.

Debtors owe all the deposit account balances back to their creditor banks, as payment of the debtors' loan account debt balances and bond debts.

As long as payees have the deposit account money supply, debtors can't pay it back.

The commercial banks' debt-based "repayable bank loan and bond purchase" deposit account money supply creation system, systematically creates unpayable debts.

If governments issued debt-free money, and paid it into every citizen's bank deposit account as a monthly un-earned income: debtors could use the new deposit account balances to pay their otherwise unpayable loan account balances.

Which would prevent the otherwise inevitable mass debtor defaults and "financial crisis".

To their credit, central banks in the UK and Europe are presently looking at issuing this kind of "helicopter money", to solve their nations' otherwise unsolvable financial crises.

But market moralists - who believe in the delusion that money is produced by the economy - insist that debtors must "produce their way out of debt": even though it is clearly the case that producing more stuff for sale does not produce any more "money" - banknotes and bank deposits.

Money is issued by the monetary system: the central-commercial banking system. Money is not produced by the productive economy.

A monetary problem - unpayable debt that is caused by the commercial banks' debt-based money supply creation monopoly;

requires a monetary solution - governments and/or central banks issue debt-free "helicopter money" to fund a general debt paydown program.

The same kind of government/central bank-issued debt-free money could also fund a basic minimum income paid monthly into every citizen's bank deposit account, which would solve the insufficient spendable incomes problem that makes producer profit arithmetically impossible without never-ending debt-financed consumer spending and debt-financed government spending.

The monetary solutions to the money problems are technically simple and would be easy to implement; and would not be inflationary.

[I described how it could be done, and why it should be done, in a booklet - *How Banks Create Money and Why Governments Should Too*; and in a longer book - *A Brief History of Financial Plunder* - that describes more of the historical consequences of the banks' debt-based money supply creation system, and the asset-secured bank loan system, that systematically transfers ownership of the money and assets into ever-fewer, ever-richer hands; and reduces everybody else to wage serfdom and debt bondage in a neo-feudal society that masquerades as a "free market economy".]

The for-profit productive economy suffers the same financial failings as the banks' debt-based money supply creation system.

Stuff is not produced for use. Stuff is produced for sale.

The purpose of production is not to provide people with the economic goods and services they need and want. The purpose of production is to sell the stuff you produced for more money than you paid out as your costs of producing it, in order to earn profits.

Profit is not earned in more stuff. Profit is earned in money. Wealth is not accumulated as warehouses full of unsold stuff. Wealth is accumulated in money. You don't get wealthy by producing and saving stuff. You get wealthy by selling the stuff and accumulating the money.

Stuff rusts and rots and becomes obsolete and worthless. Money is $numbers on banknotes and in bank accounts. $Numbers don't rot or rust. Money is never obsolete. Money is forever.

Production is a cost to productive businesses.

You don't earn money by producing stuff.

You earn money by selling the stuff for more money than you paid out as your costs of producing the stuff.

Producing stuff costs money, paying workers' wages and paying for suppliers' inputs. Selling stuff earns money: consumer spending, which is business sales revenues.

The purpose of business is to earn and accumulate money, which requires producing and selling stuff to consumers, who have to keep spending evermore money buying evermore stuff so businesses can continue producing stuff for sale and earning profits and continue accumulating money.

To accumulate money, you have to earn in sales revenues, more money than you paid out in costs, so you can earn profits and accumulate the profits as your retained earnings; your liquid capital; your money savings. Then you store the money as cash in your safe; or as deposit balances in domestic and offshore bank accounts. You don't spend the money. You don't lend the money. You don't invest the money. You keep the money. Whoopee! I'm Rich!

To get rich you have to earn more money than you spend or invest; and you have to keep the surplus money - the profits, as your money savings: your financial wealth.

If you don't earn profits - if you only earn back the same money you already had, then paid out as your costs, then earned back as your sales revenues; or worse: if you get stuck with unsold inventories and earn less money in sales revenues than you paid out in costs, and lose money - there is no point in investing your own money paying the costs of producing stuff for sale.

So businesses don't do it.

If productive businesses can't earn money profits, and are suffering money losses, businesses cut costs to stop the bleeding. Businesses lay off workers, stop buying stuff from suppliers, and stop producing more money-losing stuff for sale. Which is called a Depression.

The Depression doesn't end until somebody - the government - borrows a sh*t ton of new bank-loan money and spends it paying businesses to produce War Goods and paying people to haul those goods to other people's countries and blow them up. What!? I thought goods were so scarce that we have to treasure and preserve them at all costs!? How can blowing stuff up be good and right and true!? Mysteries of the faith...

During the War, the economy is fully employed producing War Goods sold to the government, not consumer goods sold to people. The government pays the businesses and people a sh*t ton of money for producing War Goods and blowing them up.

After the War is over, the survivors have lots of money to spend buying consumer goods - and businesses have lots of money to invest converting their factories from War Goods production to consumer goods production, and paying the costs of hiring workers and buying inputs to produce stuff for sale - so the people and businesses spend and invest the economy back to work producing consumer goods.

{And the governments who debt-financed their War spending with new bank loan money owe permanently higher total debts to the banks; and to the capital markets investors who buy the governments' debts in the secondary markets to earn the bond interest payments as their capital income.}

Until, after a decade or two, the capitalists have once again accumulated most of the money as their earned and saved profits, so consumers don't have enough money to spend buying stuff, so businesses cut back or shut down again because it is no longer possible to earn more money in sales revenues than you paid out as your costs - because your costs are consumers' spendable incomes that you pay them, which you earn back in zero-profit break even sales revenues.

In his aforementioned 1848 book, *Principles of Political Economy*, John Stuart Mill called this process of profit earning and money accumulation - followed by profitless money-losing business shutdown and Depression - the capitalist cycle. "...that such revulsions are almost periodical, is a consequence of the very tendency of profits which we are considering." {Book IV Chapter IV Section 5} ["revulsions" are what we now call recessions/Depressions; the "capitalist cycle" is now called the business cycle]

Mill was describing profit accumulation within a fixed supply money system: gold coins. But the same arithmetic applies to a zero-sum money system like commercial bank-issued credit-debt.

Commercial banks lend newly-created deposit account balances to debtors, who spend the new balances into circulation. As the loan principal payments come due, all the deposit account money must be earned back by debtors and paid back to banks and extinguished to extinguish debtors' loan account debts.

Making bank loans (and bond purchases) creates new deposit account money balances (e.g. +$1000) and equal new loan account or bond debt balances (-$1000). Repaying bank loans uncreates - extinguishes; cancels out to $0/$0 - the deposit account money balances (+$1000) and the loan account debt balances (-$1000) that were created by making the bank loans.

Credit expansion creates new spendable deposit account money and generates spending-driven prosperity. Debt paydown uncreates the money and generates Debt-Deflation Depression. {Irving Fisher, *The Debt-Deflation Theory of Great Depressions* (1933); Richard Koo called it a *Balance Sheet Recession* (2003). Koo's solution was more debt-financed government deficit spending to borrow and spend savers' money back into circulation. Fisher's solution was a government-issued money system and 100% reserve banking: *100% Money and the Public Debt* (1936)}

In Mill's gold-money scenario: The capitalists who own the productive businesses (fixed capital) start off by owning a supply of liquid capital: investible money - gold coins. You - the capitalist - pay out (invest) your gold coins to the workers and suppliers who contribute to your production of a supply of stuff for sale. The number of coins you paid out - e.g. 100 coins - is your cost price of production. But you don't sell the stuff you produce at cost price. You add markup - e.g. 10% - so you can earn more gold coins in sales revenues (110) than you paid out as your costs (100).

Let's say you produce 10 units of stuff at a cost price of 10 coins per unit: total cost price 100 coins. You add 10% markup and charge a sale price of 11 coins per unit: total projected sales revenues 110 coins.

You added 100 coins of spendable earned incomes into the economy; and you added 110 coins of payable prices into the economy.

How is it possible for consumers to spend more coins paying your prices, than the number of coins you paid them as spendable incomes?

In a fixed supply money system, the additional spending comes from consumers' savings (or from the spending of earned incomes that other producers paid out as their costs - but that just starves other producers of break-even sales revenues; or from foreigners - but that just internationalizes the money arithmetic problem without solving it).

Workers and suppliers have to spend all of the earned incomes (100 coins) that you paid out as your costs, in order for you to break even by earning back in sales revenues the same number of gold coins you paid out as your costs. You actually earn less than break even sales revenues by selling 9 units of stuff for 11 coins per unit. You paid out 100 coins and earned back 99 coins. You still have 1 unit of unsold inventory for sale for 11 coins. Somebody spends their 11 coins of savings buying that last unit of stuff, so now you have 110 gold coins, which means you earned a 10 coin profit.

You pay yourself 1 coin as a dividend, which provides you with personal spending money. You hold the 9 coin net profit as your retained earnings (savings); and you re-invest your 100 coins of "working capital" paying the costs of producing 10 more units of stuff for sale. Every other producer in the economy does the same thing: pays out spendable incomes, earns above-cost sales revenues, and accumulates profits.

But now consumers have less savings, because one saver paid you 11 coins to buy your last unit of stuff, and you are holding the 9 coin net profit out of circulation as your money savings; your accumulation of financial wealth. The saved coins are systematically transferred from consumers who spend their savings buying stuff, to producers who earn and accumulate the savings by selling the stuff at profitable prices.

Once capitalists have paid out and earned back all the gold coins - plus earned all the gold coins people already had and were saving - you and your fellow capitalists own all of *the money*; and consumers have no more savings to spend buying stuff from you. So now the only spendable money consumers have, is the same money you pay them as your present costs of producing a supply of stuff for sale. There is no point producing more stuff, just to earn back in sales revenues the same gold coins you pay out as your costs.

Break even. Zero profit. Not worth going to all the work of production, and risking loss by investing your money into a profitless market. So businesses don't invest, workers and suppliers are paid no spendable incomes, and the economy stops working.

"Establishments are shut up, or kept working without any profit, hands are discharged, and numbers of persons in all ranks, being deprived of their income, and thrown for support on their savings, find themselves, after the crisis has passed away, in a condition of more or less impoverishment."

In Mill's scenario, some of the capitalists get anxious about not investing their liquid capital and not earning any money. "...so speculations ensue, which, with the subsequent revulsions, destroy, or transfer to foreigners, a considerable amount of capital, produce a temporary rise of interest and profit, make room for fresh accumulations, and the same round is recommenced."

Capitalists accidentally lose their money, by paying it out to build or buy speculative investments, that end up losing the capitalists' money, which is gained by all the people who were paid the money, who now once again have money to spend buying stuff from other capitalists, and the same round is recommenced, until the capitalists once again earn and accumulate all the money as their profits, and the economy stops working again.

That such revulsions are almost periodical is a result of capitalists accumulating all of the spendable, investible, savable *money*. Then, like the board game Monopoly, after one player owns all the income-generating assets and owns all the money, the game of "let's have a buy-sell for money economy" ends.

But our financial lives are not ruled by the arbitrary supply of some geologically scarce metal element to make coins with. Banks can create money out of nothing and lend it to borrowers to put all the flat broke players back in the game.

Even Adam Smith - who, like his classical peers, believed gold is the only "real" money - heaped high praise on the "Scotch banks" whose credit creation increased the local circulating money supply and enabled the development of a flourishing buy-sell for money economy. {Adam Smith, *An Inquiry into the Nature and Causes of the Wealth of Nations*; Book II, Chapter II Money (1776)}

[Smith was aware of the spending-driven prosperity-generating upside of commercial bank credit creation; but was apparently unaware of the Depression-generating debt reduction downside when debtors have to earn back and extinguish the deposit account money to pay down their loan account debts. It wasn't until Irving Fisher's 1930s description of the accounting mechanics of Debt-Deflation Depressions in a bank loan money system, that this mechanism was clearly understood. I described how it works in the Boom Bust Crash chapter of the Financial Plunder book.]

Money is numbers: number of gold coins (commodity money); numbers on paper banknotes (fiat money - legal tender currency); numbers in bank deposit accounts (credit-debt money). Money works by accounting arithmetic - subtracting and adding; paying and getting paid. Money does not work by economic theories.

We do not trade stuff for other stuff in a barter-exchange economy.

We buy-sell stuff for money in a buy-sell for money economy.

The productive economy produces the stuff for sale.

The stuff is bought-sold for money in the buy-sell, spend-earn, payer-payee money economy: the financial economy.

The monetary system - the central-commercial banking system - creates the money.

Buyers of stuff (goods, services, assets) pay money to sellers of the stuff.

Paying money in a buy-sell, payer-payee transaction transfers ownership of the stuff from sellers to buyers.

The payer-payee part of the transaction transfers ownership of the money from buyers to sellers.

When one party pays money, the other party is paid the money. When one party spends or invests (pays) money, the other party earns (is paid) the money. Money spenders and money investors pay money to money earners. Payers pay money to payees. Money is the payments medium that is used to conduct all of the buy-sell, spend-earn, payer-payee money transactions.

We use the spendable banknotes and coins in our pockets; and the spendable balances in our bank deposit accounts; as our supply of spendable, investible, savable payments media: our money supply.

A spend-earn, payer-payee transaction subtracts money from the payer's personal money supply, and equally adds to the payee's personal money supply. No additional money is created by payer-payee transactions. It is a zero-sum transfer of money from one party to the other party.

Businesses are value-adding productive enterprises who add value to the inputs they buy, and produce outputs that are "worth more" than the sum of the values of the inputs. But adding *value* to the cost price of inputs does not add any additional *money* into the spend-earn money stream.

In order for businesses to get paid for the value they add, somebody has to add additional money into the spend-earn stream, so consumers can spend more money than they earn, which enables businesses to earn more money out of the stream in above-cost sales revenues (output value), than they invested into the stream as their cost price of production (input value).

"Profit" is how business owners *get paid for* the value they add into the real economy.

Debt-financed government spending; and debt-financed household spending; adds the additional new bank loan money into the spend-earn money stream that enables businesses to earn money profits and get paid for the value they added into the real economy.

[Commercial banks sell some of the interest-bearing loan account debts and bond debts into the savings-funded capital markets financial system (the "shadow banking" system), where savers pay their money (via their brokerage accounts or investment bank accounts) to buy the debts to hold as interest-earning assets - to get paid the debtors' interest payments. Savers indirectly lend their savings to fund the debtors' debt-financed spending, when savers buy the debts in the secondary markets - the capital markets.

In CH Douglas's social credit money and price system, a government monetary authority would create the additional money: which would eliminate the need for debt-financing the government deficit-spending, and would eliminate the unpayable bond debts, and would eliminate the bond interest payments.

In Milton Friedman's 1948 paper, *A Monetary and Fiscal Framework for Economic Stability*, a government monetary authority would issue money to fund government deficit spending, and extinguish money when the government had a budget surplus. Governments would no longer issue bond debts to borrow bank-issued money; and to borrow savings from capital markets investors.

Friedman stated: The government should always issue, never borrow, its deficit-spending money. The debt-free government money spending would add the needed money into the spend-earn stream, which enables producer profits and money accumulation, without requiring ever-increasing - and permanently unpayable - household and government debt.

It was also Friedman who observed (in 1969) that the central bank could always end a deflationary Depression by printing money and dropping it out of helicopters. People would pick up the free "helicopter money" and spend moribund businesses back to work producing stuff for sale to earn the renewed money spending.

CH Douglas and Irving Fisher (in the 1930s), and Milton Friedman (in 1948), all advocated the radical monetary system reform of converting from a commercial bank-issued money system; to a 100% government-issued money system and 100% reserve banking. In 2012, two IMF research economists - Jaromir Benes and Michael Kumhof - revived and updated Fisher's radical monetary reform proposal in their paper, *The Chicago Plan Revisited*.

But no such reforms have ever been implemented, anywhere, with the possible exception of China whose national government owns the central bank and owns the big State commercial banks and uses the banks' money issuing function as the monetary-fiscal (money creation and allocation) arm of China's economic and industrial policy.]

Like the board game Monopoly, banks supply all the money that is used in the real world buy-sell for money economy. But unlike the game Monopoly, banks do not start the game by "giving" each player a supply of money. Banks "lend" the money to the players, and the players owe all the money back to the banks. Repaying bank loans uncreates the deposit account money. Meanwhile, as long as borrowers' bank loans and bond debts remain unpaid, the economy has a supply of bank-issued money to use, to conduct all of its payer-payee money transactions.

As population increases and the buy-sell for money economy grows, the economy needs a bigger circulating money supply to enable all the buy-sell, spend-earn money transactions; and a bigger total money supply to accommodate payees earning and accumulating money as their savings - without starving the economy's spend-earn stream of its *circulating* money supply by savers earning money out of the stream then holding the money out of circulation as their accumulations of financial wealth.

A growing population with a growing buy-sell for money economy needs a growing money supply to conduct all of its buy-sell transactions and to earn and accumulate as savings. It needs "more money".

Gold coins are made "out of gold", which has to be discovered somewhere on Earth, then mined and refined and minted into coins. If you run out of "more gold", you can't make "more money".

But central banks can create more banknotes by printing numbers on slips of paperlike material; and commercial banks can create more bank deposits by typing numbers in bank deposit accounts. Hurray! Banks can create money "out of nothing", to save us all from monetary scarcity imposed by the barbarous relic gold!

...or scarcity of "circulating" money imposed by capitalists' accumulation of the money supply as their retained earnings; their savings; their earned and saved profits; their investible - but not invested - "capital". There is plenty of money, but it has been earned and accumulated by "the rich", who save most of their money, or invest it buying financial assets like stocks and bonds, or buying real assets like rental real estate.

Assets generate capital incomes. Stocks pay dividend income. Bonds pay interest income. Rental real estate pays rental income. You earn capital incomes by *owning* income-generating assets.

Rich people spend their money buying assets from other rich people. Buyers pay money to sellers. The rich buyer now owns the assets; the rich seller now owns the money. Rich people *own* most of the income-generating assets, and most of the investible money; and most of the savings.

[Unless you own $10s of millions of money and assets, you know you are not actually "rich". $1 million of personal savings invested buying stocks and bonds that yield 2% annual return earns you a not-so-princely annual income of $20,000. To earn $100,000 of (before tax) capital income in a 2% yield environment, you need to own $5 million of investment assets. "Being a millionaire" no longer makes you rich. But compared to *everybody else* on this money-poor planet, you are "the rich" if you own just a few 100 thousand dollars of investment assets and investible money.]

There is plenty of money spending-earning and buying-selling in the assets markets. Asset yields are at historic lows because asset prices are at historic highs. Asset prices are inflated by the global "glut" of investible savings that adds buy-money into the assets markets, which enables asset owners to ask - and get paid - higher prices for selling their assets.

There is no scarcity of investible money circulating among rich people - and rich corporations - who buy-sell assets in the assets markets. There is no shortage of personal and corporate savings account balances in domestic and offshore bank accounts.

There is a scarcity of buying-selling and money spending-earning in the "real" producer-consumer economy where money-poor people get paid money for working, then spend their incomes paying their costs of living and buying consumer goods and services. Spendable consumer incomes are a declining fund, because the "rich" capitalists who own the productive businesses earn and accumulate the spent money as savable, investible profits - which starves the producer-consumer economy's spend-earn money stream of its circulating *money supply*.

So the banks step in and offer credit to consumers, so consumers can spend more money than they earn by debt-financing their additional spending; and businesses can earn the borrowed-and-spent money as their profits. Hallelujah! For-profit market economy is saved by the banks!

But debt has to be paid back out of future earned incomes - which businesses will pay out as their future costs. Consumers' earned incomes = producers' cost price. Governments tax and redistribute the re-spending of the earned incomes; but tax-and-redistribute does not add any additional money into the economy's spend-earn money stream. The only income-money in the stream - that can be used to buy stuff and paydown debts - is the money producers invested into the stream as their cost price of production.

If consumers spend less money than they earn, because they are using their incomes to pay down their debts, then producers will earn below-cost sales revenues and will suffer money losses.

So businesses will stop investing their money in profitless money losing production, and there will be a Depression. Businesses will lay off workers, stop buying stuff from suppliers, and shut down or cut back to stop bleeding more of the owners' money.

[So newly shut down businesses and newly-unemployed workers will not be earning any incomes to make their bank loan payments, so there will be mass debtor defaults that bankrupt the creditor banks, who are saved by taxpayer funded bailouts; and by central bank liquidity injections; and by regulatory forbearance that does not require insolvent banks to "recognize" their balance sheet insolvency - because recognition would require resolution by bank bankruptcies (like the 1930s)...

...which ends by bankruptcy Trustees writing off catastrophic amounts of our 'money in the bank' as bankrupt banks' unpayable *deposit liability debts*. Or ends by regulators bailing in, and banks writing off, apocalyptic amounts of our deposit account balances, to restore solvency to banks' balance sheets by writing off trillions of the banks' unpayable deposit liability debts. Either way - bank bankruptcies or depositor bail-ins - our 'money in the bank' gets written off.

Rich people - very rich people - have their savings tucked away in "offshore" bank accounts (or in cryptocurrency accounts like Bitcoin), safely out of reach of bankruptcy writeoffs and depositor bail-ins. Rich people's savings will not be written off. Poor people have no savings. Middle class savings will be written off. Ownership of the money will be concentrated in even-fewer, even-richer hands; while middle class savers - who earned their money by working their small-medium businesses, or by working as well paid professionals, not by owning assets - get poorer. That is: money earning workers get poorer; asset owning capitalists get richer. Do we see a pattern developing here?

Central bank liquidity injections can restore liquidity to illiquid banks' reserve accounts; but that does not restore solvency to insolvent banks' balance sheets. That's the problem the Dodd-Frank debt-for-equity swaps program will solve, by bailing in and writing off our 'money in the bank'.

Government issuance of debt-free helicopter money - paid into every citizen's bank deposit account as a monthly un-earned income - makes debtors' unpayable loan account debts payable, which makes banks' uncollectable interest-earning assets collectable, which makes banks' unpayable deposit liability debts payable, which prevents balance sheet insolvency, which eliminates the need to write off our 'money in the bank'.

But that beneficial outcome requires breaking the banks' longstanding monopoly of debt-based money issuance. And so far, no nation (with the possible exception of China) has managed to do that.]

Debt-financed spending enables consumers to spend more money than they earn today, which enables producers to earn profits today.

But debt has to be repaid out of future earned incomes, which are producers' future costs.

When the future arrives and debtors start spending their earned incomes paying down debts instead of buying the stuff businesses produce for sale, businesses will earn less money in sales revenues than they paid out as their costs, and will lose money instead of earning profits, so they shut down again and there is the next Depression.

Debt-financed consumer spending robs the future to pay the present. When the future arrives and the debts have to be paid down, the spending-driven economy descends into Debt-Deflation Depression.

Which is solved by the fiscal stimulus of another War!!! which permits governments to declare Damn the budget! and borrow a sh*t ton of money and spend it paying their businesses and citizens to blow sh*t up.

Then in the next post-War cycle the capitalists again accumulate most of the money as their profits, and there is the next Depression.

Until the Pandemic!!! changes everything: first by globalist 'health' authorities shutting down the economy entirely; then by central banks creating trillions of new money and giving it to all the too big to fail commercial and shadow banks and industrial and commercial corporations; and finally by central banks creating trillions of new helicopter money for governments to give to people as an un-earned - but spendable - income: so the people can pay their bank loans and can once again become good and faithful consumers who spend the dead-in-the-water economy back to work producing stuff for sale; and capitalists can resume producing stuff and selling it at above-cost prices to consumers, so capitalists can resume earning profits and accumulating money.

As long as the "free money" keeps being created out of nothing and given to consumers and spent into the economy and earned and accumulated by capitalists, everybody lives happily ever after...

...except the Earth and the biosphere, which is scarified for resources to produce materials that businesses can convert into more stuff for sale, while dumping all the toxic pollution into the soil and water and air and oceans.

And the "creative destruction" of dumping all last year's stuff into garbage dumps to make room for all the new stuff that has to be sold this year to maintain sales revenues and profits and prevent the buy-sell for money producer-consumer economy from descending into Depression again.

As long as money is issued for profit, not for use; and as long as stuff is produced for profit, not for use; there is no way out of this doom cycle clusterf*ck.

As long as "new and improved!" is not replaced by "old and still works; and is fixable", Earth's environment and biosphere is f*cked.

And so are we, whose lives depend on the life of this planet.

As long as stuff is built to be replaced, not built to last - because businesses need to produce and sell more stuff to survive as for-profit financial entities - there is no way of reducing our industrial scale wastage of what remains of the Earth's natural resources and accessible energy resources.

As long as electric-powered and fossil fuel-powered machines continue to do an ever-increasing share of the physical work of production and transportation; and as long as fossil-fueled corporate agribusiness continues to mass produce the chemical fertilized, pesticide saturated, heavily processed foodlike substances that feed the hungry masses - while humans get fat and weak and sick from unhealthy food, unhealthy lifestyle, and physical inactivity in a machine-polluted environment - humans are engaged in industrial scale suicide.

As long as production is "globalized" and dominated by transnational corporate monopolists who own and operate "the economy" as their private corporate fiefdoms, there will be no productive work for the redundant masses of serfs whose labor-free lives in Consumer Paradise are killing them.

The technocrats' wet dream will be realized. Social Darwinists won't have to rationalize the moral evil of deliberately killing off the redundant billions. The billions are killing themselves, by exercising their inalienable right as Almighty Consumers to enjoy their physically comfortable labor-free consumer lifestyle, brought to a planet near you by smart technocrats showcasing their smart labor-saving technologies, sold to you by smart marketers who tell you that you are Almighty and who know how to push your "gotta buy it" buttons, and debt-financed by your friendly neighborhood transnational goliath banking corporation who invites you to borrow and spend your way into inescapable debt bondage.

I will end this elegy here, rather than continue describing the gathering sh*tstorm of doom cycle clusterf*cks that are in the process of Collapsing the capitalist-owned for-profit industrial civilization that we have come to know and love and depend on for our ongoing survival as mindless debt-financed buyers of whatever planet-destroying and life-destroying corporate-produced baubles the marketers are selling this week.

Requiem

Is it really that hopeless?

Probably.

But maybe not.

People made this world.

People can change it, by making different choices, by abandoning the myopically materialistic market economy worldview and adopting a different set of beliefs about who and what we are and why we are here; and a different set of values about what we "should" be doing here.

But "the people" can't change it.

People have power to change ourselves: learn; change our own minds; change our individual lives.

But the people have no power to change the world, the culture, the collective way of life.

Rulers rule the world: decide what will be done, and what will not be done.

But the rulers themselves are ruled by Money, whose magical workings mystify the rulers and bind them.

Money is numbers that are created out of nothing, but our financial and economic lives depend on money accounting arithmetic.

If you invest 1000 as your costs, then earn 1100 in sales revenues, you recover your 1000 of investible capital in break even sales revenues, and you earn 100 profit as your own spendable, savable income, and you survive to invest another day as a for-profit financial enterprise. If you invest 1000, then earn 900 in sales revenues, you lose 100 of your own money, and you soon run out of your own money to lose in your producing stuff for sale business. So you shut down the money-losing abomination.

It makes no difference that you were producing real stuff that people need and want. It makes no difference how much "economic" value you were adding into the real world. In buy-sell for money market economy that uses bank-issued debt-based money and works by money accounting arithmetic, only money "counts", and money-losing entities must surely die.

Our lives are ruled by Almighty $Numbers.

Money is the central feature and the most basic necessity of our economic lives and livelihoods.

We work to get paid money. We produce stuff to sell for money. We buy everything we need and want from "the economy", and we pay with money.

Everybody needs money.

By offering to pay enough money you can motivate people to build, make, produce, think, do, say, pretty much everything that is within human power to do.

Money commands human action.

By offering to pay enough money you can buy ownership of everything in the world that can be bought-sold for money. Pretty much everything - including the water you drink, the food you eat, and the ground you are standing on - has been converted to "property" that is bought-sold for money.

Money buys ownership of the Earth.

Money is the command and control system that activates and directs the money-using world; and distributes ownership.

Whoever issues the money decides who gets how much of the newly created money, for what purposes.

Banks, not governments, issue the money supply of nations.

The nations are ruled by bankers who decide how much money they will create and lend to the people, businesses and governments, for what purposes, at what cost in interest, and on what repayment terms.

The world is not ruled by Presidents and Prime Ministers and Kings who slouch into the marketplace clutching interest-bearing bond debts which they hope to sell to bankers to borrow bank-issued money to spend.

As a non-negotiable condition of the loans, the bankers - the creditors - dictate the fiscal austerity policies by which governments must increase taxes and reduce spending to generate budget surpluses - the government version of "profits" - that the governments can pay to bankers (and to capital markets investors) as interest on the ever-increasing, permanently unpayable National Bond Debt.

When governments inevitably default on paying their unpayable bond debts, governments are compelled to sell the public infrastructure - at debt-distressed prices far below what it cost to build the infrastructure - to get money to pay the delinquent bond interest payments, without paying down any of the loan principal debt.

The public infrastructure - roads, ports and airports, water and sewer systems, electrical and telecommunications systems, schools - becomes privatized infrastructure: an income-generating asset that is used to produce profits for its new private owners.

Debt-financed development systematically transfers ownership of assets out of the hands of the people, businesses and nations who built them by working, into the hands of the creditors who debt-financed them with money that banks create out of nothing.

Most of the people who work in government, just like the market moralists, do not know banks create money out of nothing. The elected members of governments believe money is somehow produced by the economy, so they can only get money by collecting taxes out of the economy; or by borrowing savings from the economy by issuing interest-bearing bond debts to borrow money from the money merchants in the money markets.

"Your merchants were the world's great men.

By your magic spell all the nations were led astray." (Revelation 18:23)

Money - Almighty $Numbers - is the Biblical Whore of Babylon by whose intoxicating wine the Kings of the Earth are lured into servitude and brought to utter destruction. (Revelation Chapters 17, 18)

The hearts of the "elders and leaders of the people" have been corrupted with love of Money and all it can buy; and their minds have been polluted with the life-destroying, planet-destroying ideological and moral "certainties" of market economy and market morality.

Though they exercise the power to create money out of nothing, bankers are not free either. To survive as for-profit financial enterprises, banks must collect more money out of the world (loan principal + interest payments) than they created and loaned into the world (loan principal).

It is logically and arithmetically impossible, but they have to do it anyway, because the money issuers are just as bound by the implacable dictates of Almighty $Numbers as is everybody else in this money using world.

We all live in servitude to the impossible demands of the Whore of Babylon.

And we will continue to live in servitude until the Whore's magic spell is broken and governments wake up and see that they can issue their own money (like Benjamin Franklin and Abraham Lincoln did); and see that they can issue money to pay for money-losing but socially, economically, environmentally and financially beneficial public goods.

Like cleaning up the environment. And paying people a basic income so they can pay their cost of living spending and pay down their bank loan debts.

And until governments see that by issuing their own money to pay incomes to the people and businesses who produce the money-losing public goods and provide the money-losing public services, the government provides the private sector economy with a "money supply" to use to conduct its own buying and selling, investing and earning, paying and getting paid. And to earn and accumulate as savings, without starving debtors of debt repayment money, because the money was not issued as "loans", so the government-issued money supply is not owed "back" to anybody.

I'm going to agree with Isaiah and the old school prophets.

The human world is populated with many sheep and few shepherds.

The people are sheep, dependent on their shepherds to lead them to green pastures and still waters, not lead them to the fleecing floors and slaughterhouses.

The shepherds - the elders and leaders of the people - can be informed by enlightened reason and guided by moral virtue to serve the interests of life, humanity, and the planet.

Or the shepherds can be corrupted by perverse ideology that encourages and justifies their beastly lust to gain power, wealth and privilege at everybody else's expense.

Are we spiritual, moral beings who have higher purposes? Are we citizens of Enlightened nations who rationally understand our situation and cooperate toward our mutual benefit?

Are we greedy physical beasts driven by our animal lusts? Are we competitors in market economy who destroy each other - and the world we live in - to win battles and claw our way up power and wealth hierarchies?

We are both. Which side dominates within a person and within a society depends on which one is fed and encouraged, and which one is starved and suppressed. Feed the beast and you get beast society. Feed the spiritual nature - and suppress the beast - and you get human society.

The shepherds and the sheep believe in and live by whichever version of human nature and human society the authorities - the intellectual priesthood - choose to present as real, and which to dismiss as impossible illusion; which to promote as virtuous and constructive, and which to condemn as destructive and morally wrong.

In our world, the most "successful" of the professional intellectuals - the economists - have sold their souls to market economy's owning class, to get paid for being "the authorities" who invent the plausible-sounding "this is what the world is like" narratives that obfuscate the beastly actions - and justify the power, wealth and privilege - of the corrupt rulers.

Though the empirical content of the narratives is often directly contradicted by the visible evidence of reality, the ideological narratives become "the facts" - the conventional wisdom - the certainty of whose objective truth is beyond doubt or question within the "authoritative consensus" that establishes what is true and good and right, and what is not.

It becomes the job of the intellectual priesthood to preach the conventional wisdom and defend its truth-claims by reciting the facile but appealing slogans - you can't stop progress! even better jobs! - that function as the ideology's "facts".

Any intellectual who fails to recite the conventional wisdom with sufficiently authoritative certainty is suspected of being an unbeliever. Any intellectual who dares to question the truth of the delusory truth-claims - upon which rock the entire ideological edifice of the dominant worldview is built - is stripped of their priestly status as an "authority" and cast into the outer darkness for their blasphemous heresies against the authoritative consensus.

The honest, uncorrupted intellectuals - such as what remains of the old style investigative journalists and scientific researchers and economists who see and tell the truth in direct contradiction to the authoritative narratives - are dismissed by the authorities as "deniers" and conspiracy theorist nutjobs.

People - the innocent sheep - believe in the authorities who talk on TV and hate the nutjob conspiracy theorists who are trying to open the sheeps' eyes and destroy the comforting delusions the sheep are dreaming as they're driven dreamily to the slaughterhouse.

The rulers of market economy are themselves induced to believe in the ideological claptrap and mythical histories they pay the intellectuals to think up and pay the corporate-owned mass media talking heads to disseminate.

Many of the shepherds are just as brain-addled with false certainties and morally manipulated by heroic mythical narratives as are the sheep.

Many members of the intellectual priesthood themselves come to believe that the Emperor's new ideology - their made up narratives and consensus beliefs and theories - is "objective truth"; or worse...objective *reality*.

I will mimic Isaiah, and Jesus: Woe unto the High Priests who curry favor and gain fortune and authority by blaspheming against the Spirit of truth to lead the whole world astray.

The world that the sheep inhabit depends on which world the shepherds create.

The moral blame for what ails humanity has never resided with the innocent sheep who go where they are led.

It has always resided with the not so good shepherds who lead the sheep astray.

The morally corrupted world Isaiah condemned is the same world we inhabit today.

It is a classic Greek tragedy, where the strong-willed and ambitious doers are driven by their powerlust and emboldened by their ideological arrogance and moralistic certainties to make themselves the leaders who destroy themselves and everyone who has the misfortune to be swept along in the calamitous whirlwind of their blindly misguided hubris.

It is these - the self-appointed shepherds who lead the human flock to doom or salvation - who must see with their eyes, hear with their ears, understand with their hearts, and turn, and be healed.

2600 years after Isaiah preached it, it still hasn't happened.

But this time is different, right?

Bibliography

Benes, Jaromir and Kumhof, Michael; *The Chicago Plan Revisited* (2012)

Douglas, CH; *Money and the Price System* (1935)

Fisher, Irving; *The Debt-Deflation Theory of Great Depressions* (1933)

Fisher, Irving; *100% Money and the Public Debt* (1936)

Friedman, Milton; *A Monetary and Fiscal Framework for Economic Stability* (1948)

Koo, Richard; *Balance Sheet Recession* (2003)

Marx, Karl and Engels, Friedrich; *The Communist Manifesto* (1848)

Mill, John Stuart; *Principles of Political Economy* (1848)

Moore, Michael and Gibbs, Jeff; *Planet of the Humans* (2020)

Polanyi, Karl; *The Great Transformation: The Political and Economic Origins of Our Time* (1944)

Ricardo, David; *Principles of Political Economy and Taxation* (1817)

Smith, Adam; *An Inquiry into the Nature and Causes of the Wealth of Nations* (1776)

The Bible: New International Version

www.ingramcontent.com/pod-product-compliance
Lightning Source LLC
Chambersburg PA
CBHW050309220526
45465CB00005B/1919